PEACE, be still.

James Edward Burks

Peace, be still.

By James Edward Burks

Peace, be still.
Copyright © 2024 James Edward Burks

Printed by:
Kindle Direct Publishing, an Amazon.com Company

All rights reserved. The author grants you permission to reproduce or translate parts of this book without altering the content.

All scripture references are the King James Version
unless otherwise noted.

ISBN: 979-8-9897764-2-9

Cover Design by:
His Workmanship, LLC - www.hisworkmanship-LLC.com

Book Dedication

With these written words, I honor the Father, Son and Holy Spirit, for He is the true author and finisher of this work. I dedicate this book to everyone who has ever faced a storm in life. As of this writing, many are dealing with the aftermath of Hurricanes Helene and Milton in the United States. We are seeing firsthand how devastating a storm can be. I'm writing to not only encourage them, but to also come alongside the countless number of people who have and are battling storms that are deep within and need to hear the Lord speak into these storms,
"Peace, be still."

Special Thanks

I am grateful for the opportunity to minister through
One Voice Ministries, Inc., and I appreciate all the people who support what we do. I'm grateful for opportunities and projects like this.
It is my way of 'preaching on paper'.

I am forever grateful for the love of my incredibly supportive helpmate, my wife, Heather Anne Burks, and for her edits on this project.
Also, a special thank you to my friend and sister in Christ,
Tammy Dezonno-Toby, who shared audio recordings of me from years of sermons during a season in which I was blessed to be her Pastor. These messages, given by the Holy Spirit, serve as the launchpad for the core thoughts behind this and other future works.

Special Dedication

In the final stages of publishing this book, my family encountered a sudden and unexpected storm, the passing of my brother-in-love, Kevin Johns. One of the last things we did together was he and his wife, my sister-in-love, Robin, came and stayed with us to ride out Hurricane Milton. To Robin, and their children Ben and Katie, we love you and we will remain here with you to ride out this storm. My prayer for you is that you experience God's grace and perfect love in the days ahead, and for you to hear Jesus whisper, "Peace, be still" over the waves of this storm.

Table of Contents

Book Dedication and Special Thanks……..……………………………...……..4

Prologue ………………………………....………………………………....…..6

Chapter One
Some Fell Among Thorns…………………..…..…………..……......13

Chapter Two
A Grain of Mustard Seed ……………..…..…………………..……18

Chapter Three
Let Us Pass Over unto The Other Side………………………………..21

Chapter Four
A Great Storm of Wind…………………………………………….....25

Chapter Five
Asleep on a Pillow……………………………………………………30

Chapter Six
Peace, be still……………………………………………………….…35

Chapter Seven
Why Are Ye So Fearful……………………………………………..…40

Chapter Eight
The Other Side of The Sea…………………………………...………..45

Chapter Nine
My Peace I Give unto You…………………………..…………………50

Chapter Ten
The Peace of God and Peace with God………………………...……..53

Epilogue …………………………………………………..…….……..56

Prologue

Usually, the prologue of a book is used to give context to the story, set the mood of the writing, or to present background information or a foreshadowing of things to come later. As I was praying about this manuscript, this is the thought that came in my spirit. As I am attempting to offer insight into God's Word for the benefit of the reader, what I share lacks purpose and effectiveness without the reader being pulled towards the source of the power that makes these words true. So, please bear with me as I share a message that I pray will draw you and connect you with the one true God, Jesus Christ, and how salvation through His sacrifice has been made possible for you. Please feel free to copy this prologue and share it with anyone you believe would benefit from reading it and hearing it in their heart and spirit. "Faith cometh by hearing and hearing by the word of God." Romans 10:17 KJV

Who, What, Why, Where, When… and How

Growing up in school we used a method of gathering, analyzing and organizing information called the 5W's. I've arranged them in a particular order, and added "how", to help you assemble what you need to make a life changing decision.

Who

The "who" at the center of everything that is important is God. Not any random 'god' that exists in many forms and covers every variation of belief, but the one true God of the Holy Bible. God is the Creator of all existence and is the sustainer of the universe, who revealed himself to us through the scripture as the triune God: Father, Son, and Spirit. God has always existed and started the human time clock, not with a 'bang', but His words. Genesis, the first book of the Bible, in the first verse, states that "In the beginning God created the heavens and the earth" which indicated that to start something you must proceed its inception. He said, "let there be", and everything manifested into reality. What we know about the triunity of God was put on display during the work of creation. The Father, spoke and the Word, Jesus (John chapter 1) created all things, and the Spirit moved over and throughout the process.

On the 6th day of creation, God made man in His image and likeness. Genesis clarifies that God created male and female… only. He brought them together to be fruitful, multiply, and have dominion over all of creation. Man was given the freedom to choose to submit to God's plan and directives or decide not to, but remember, choices have consequences. Influenced by a fallen angel, Lucifer, better known as Satan, the choice man made to rebel and reject God's plan ushered in the existence of sin. Therefore man, and consequently all of mankind, fell away and came short of God's glory and standard. The perfection of creation was destroyed, even the earth itself suffered the effects of sin. A remedy was necessary to restore what was broken.

What

Now that man's heart was filled with sin and his thoughts and intentions were evil, the solution had to come from the only remaining perfection, God himself. Since a human was responsible for this catastrophe, God took on human flesh Himself, in the form of Jesus Christ, the only begotten son, to do for us what we couldn't. What God did was enter His own creation by a virgin birth, grow up as a child, and minister as a man. The Son of man was also the Son of God, but for us he set aside His divine authority and humbled himself as a servant, subject to the will of His Father and filled with the Spirit of God. He came as prophesied in the Old Testament as a sheep to be slaughtered to be the perfect sacrifice and pay the penalty for our violation (sin) against God's commands. What He did while walking the earth was to heal the sick, raise the dead, give sight to the blind, feed the hungry, love and bless the children, in all, exampling for us what our new relationship with the Father would be like through Him.

When a rebellion occurs against the King, there is a penalty and price that must be paid by the perpetrators of this uprising. According to scripture, the price or the "wages" to be paid for sin is death (Romans 6:23). The price to be paid was death. To cover all the sins of mankind; past, present, and future, only Jesus could satisfy that demand. The perfection of Jesus was the only sufficient offering to change our eternal circumstance. Jesus was willing to lay down His life, in other words, He allowed Himself to be crucified by men and punished by God, for every sin you and I and everyone everywhere for all time have ever committed. His blood was shed, and His life given so that you and I could be set free from our punishment and be redeemed and forgiven.

The saving power of the sacrifice Jesus made on the cross was not only in His death, but also in His resurrection. Having considered His offering sufficient as a payment for the sins of all people for all time, the Father raised Jesus from the dead, to never die again. Romans 6: 9 and 10 reads, "Knowing that Christ being raised from the dead dieth no more; death hath no more dominion over him. For in that he died, he died unto sin once: but in that he liveth, he liveth unto God."

So, Jesus died and rose again to save us, forgive us and redeem us. This is the gospel… the 'good news' for us all. It is a gospel we should rejoice in and never be ashamed of. It is good news that God revealed His righteousness through and the object of our faith for us to live by. Romans 1:16-17 says, "For I am not ashamed of the gospel of Christ: for it is the power of God unto salvation to every one that believeth; to the Jew first, and also to the Greek. For therein is the righteousness of God revealed from faith to faith: as it is written, The just shall live by faith."

Why

Why would He do that? Why would he allow the Father's full wrath to be poured out on Himself? Maybe the better question is why would the Father not spare His own son? Why would He allow him to be beaten and tortured and hung on a cross, experiencing unthinkable pain and unimaginable suffering… just for me… just for you? A verse of scripture familiar to many, John 3:16 explains it well. It says, "For God so loved the world…" let's pause there for a moment. God's motivation for offering Himself for us is His deep abiding love for us. He loves you so much that no cost was too high, no suffering too great that He wouldn't do whatever it took to make a way for you to be restored and return to the relationship He created you to have. Any good father would pay the ultimate price to save his child, and that's what He did for us.

To fully understand His love, you must keep in mind, He didn't do this because we deserved it, or earned it, or were even capable of asking for it. The Bible said that "while we were yet sinners", not because we were even turning to the right direction, He died on our behalf to make things right between us and Himself. Back to John 3:16, He "so loved" us, His love was so deep and so immense towards us, "that He gave His only begotten Son". His love action was a gift to us. The risk of offering a gift is that the one it is being offered to is not required to accept it. Can you imagine the degree and depth of His love to put it all on the table knowing it might still be rejected by the ones He did it for. The good thing is that God received the sacrifice as sufficient to pay the cost required for our forgiveness. To prove that, three days later, Christ rose from the dead, literally came back to life with and by the power of God... all power! Keep in mind the Father's love is so great towards us that even though we sinned against Him, He is the one that draws us to salvation (John 6:44). Imagine that the very one who will punish sin, gave His Son to give us a way out of the punishment of sin. God is both just and the justifier.

Where

So, the question I have to ask is, 'Where are you?' Because of sin and the sin nature we all inherited from Adam, we are all broken and separated from God. We all deserve the punishment of eternal separation from God in a place the Bible calls hell because of our self-will and rebellion against the King of Glory. It was meant for Satan and his defectors, but it will become the place of all who choose to follow Satan right to their grave. Please understand, it doesn't end here. After this earthly life is over, we will all have to answer to our Creator and King for our choice to reject and commit treason against Him. And that will lead to our separation from Him for ever more.

The greatest question we will have to give an account of will be how we responded to the gift being offered by His Son Jesus, and whether we trusted Him to be our Savior and rescue and save our life from the deserved punishment that awaited us. Also, did we willingly surrender our lives to Him to be Lord to lead, guide, and direct us daily? Was there work that followed salvation that honored and exalted Jesus as King and Master of our life or did we operate in a prideful, self-serving manner having not truly surrendered to Jesus at all? Did your heart truly belong to Him, walking in obedience to His Word and believing them to be absolute truth or was it all an act and we just pretended to be spiritual to impress and win favor with man?

Where are you right now? Are you still attempting to be the one in control of your life, or have you given your life fully to Him? Are you still trying to convince yourself that you are a good enough person and basically decent while managing things yourself, or do you completely understand the total depravity of your darkened heart and recognize that apart from Christ you can do nothing of worth or value? I know that sounds harsh, and even hurtful, which may cause many to push away from God's loving offer. But it is only when you embrace the truth of who and what you are without Jesus that you can truly see your need for Him and turn from sin and believe who He is and what He did for you.

When

Having heard of God's love and sacrifice for you and recognized your need, my last question is when are you going to do something about this in your heart? When are you going to repent and believe? When are you going to surrender and be saved? When are you going to trust and obey? When are you going to lay your life at His feet and cry out for forgiveness? How about right now? Maybe the reason you are reading this book, maybe the reason someone shared it with you, was for this very moment, for just such a time as this. I know we'd all like to think we have an endless amount of time and will all live to a ripe old age and therefore we have time to make this decision and change. I'm not trying to use fear as a scare tactic, but the simple reality is we don't know how much time we have to make a decision about our eternity, but we must choose, and by not choosing, essentially the choice is made. There is no neutral ground. You are either seeking Christ or denying Christ. What I do know is that if God has stirred your heart through these words, because only the Father draws us to Himself, the "when" can be right now.

The offering of salvation is an offer of God's mercy. He tells us in Isaiah 55 verses 6 through 8 that we should, "Seek the Lord while he may be found, call ye upon him while he is near: Let the wicked forsake his way, and the unrighteous man his thoughts: and let him return unto the Lord, and he will have mercy upon him; and to our God, for he will abundantly pardon. For my thoughts are not your thoughts, neither are your ways my ways, saith the Lord." What thoughts and what ways? His mercy and grace. His truth and love. As undeserving and rebellious as we are, God's heart is to have mercy on us, He loves us that much. Have you ever had a difficult time forgiving an offense towards you? Do you wrestle with releasing someone from a hurt or sting, feeling that the person doesn't deserve to be let off the hook because of what they did? God doesn't think that way. He operates in the truth that our sins require punishment, but he also operates in a love that wants to pour out his mercy on us to forgive us of those very same sins.

How

How do we abandon our ways and thoughts? How do we find freedom from the deserved consequences of our sin? The Bible says that "if we confess with our mouth the Lord Jesus (or that Jesus is Lord of our life) and believe in our heart that God has raised Him from the dead, you shall be saved." Romans 10:9. Repentance and belief is what is required for salvation. Baptism comes later, joining a Christian fellowship comes later, reading your bible comes later, but it begins with repenting (turn away from sin, self and Satan) and believing who Jesus is (God in the flesh) and what he did to secure your salvation (died a sacrificial death on the cross taking God's wrath for your sins). We must be completely convinced that He suffered, died and rose again for all of us and by surrendering your life and will to Him, this will allow you to be saved and forgiven by His unmerited grace through that faith you have placed in him.

Once you have repented and believed in the finishing work of the cross and the reality of Christ's lordship, here is the effect and outcome of what happens to you and in you according to scripture: you have receive the only true salvation (Acts 4:12); you are saved (Acts 16:31); you receive the gift of God (Ephesians 2:9); you are made alive in Christ (1 Corinthians 15:22); you are made a light to the unbelievers (Acts 13:47); in you, the gospel becomes the power of God (Romans 1:16); you are reconciled by Christ's death and saved by his life (Romans 5:10); Christ becomes your strength and your refuge (Psalm 62:7); you are given everlasting life (John 3:16); you have new life because of the Son (1 John

5:12); you receive a new heart (Ezekiel 36:26); you are granted abundant life (John 10:10); your transgressions are removed (Psalm 103:12); you are washed in regeneration and renewed in the Spirit (Titus 3:5); you are redeemed and forgiven (Colossians 1:14); you are blessed (Psalm 3:8); you are chosen, a royal priesthood, part of a holy nation and a peculiar people, as well as being called into light (1 Peter 2:9); you become the righteousness of God (2 Corinthians 5:21); you died with Him and are raised with Him to sit in heavenly places (Ephesians 2:6); we become fellow citizens with the saints and the household of God (Ephesians 2:19); and we are reconciled to God (Ephesians 2:16) .

Take a moment to really take all that in. I beg you to make a decision to get before God and express your sorrow for sin and your need for Him. I won't give you a script to repeat or prayer to pray. I firmly believe that when your response is true, genuine, and the brokenness is real provoking godly sorrow, God will you give you what to say to express your heart and love towards Him. At that moment, the Spirit of God will take up residence in you and you will be forever changed, salvation is granted, and the sanctifying transformation has begun.

If you have already honestly trusted the Lord for forgiveness and redemption, then my prayer is that this prologue served as an encouragement and reminder of the assurance of your salvation, a gift you desire to share with others. If this shared gospel has impacted you to make a needed change. Or has awakened you to the fact that maybe what you thought you had secured wasn't true salvation and caused you to pray in this moment to receive Him… praise the Lord and congratulations! Now that the table is set, I pray the rest of this manuscript feeds your heart, mind, soul, and spirit as God would direct and lead.

"Father, please grant the reader of this, your work, all that you have placed in this message to illuminate and give revelation about you and your love for them. Lord, I thank you for continuing, by your grace, the sanctifying work of transforming us more into the likeness and image of your Son, Jesus. This we humbly ask, Amen."

Resting in Him,

James

Chapter One

Some Fell Among Thorns

"And some fell among thorns, and the thorns grew up, and choked it, and it yielded no fruit." Mark 4:7

Let me begin by saying that all of God's word is good, but Mark chapter 4 is filled to the point of running over with amazing teaching from Jesus. I encourage you to pause and grab your bible and go read Mark 4 and then come back. When you come back, bring your bible. Because any writing by Christian authors will always be subordinate to the Word of God. As a human, although I desire not to, I may fail or come up short, but God's Word is infallible. Never place any text above the scripture or do any study of God apart from His Word.

Having read it you will understand that I won't be able to cover that chapter in its entirety. Plus, my main theme is later in the chapter concerning what happened on the boat with Jesus. But I had to give you a little appetizer of some of the early parts of this chapter. So, Jesus is teaching by the sea and so many people came that He got in a ship on the water. Jesus understood aquatic acoustics and that the downward refraction of sound over water allows you to hear better. Yes, I looked up that explanation, but Jesus knew it because he created both water and sound.

> *"...your depth in Christ will reflect your growth in Christ."*

On this occasion, He taught what we often refer to as the Parable of the Sower. A quick review: a man went out to sow or plant seeds. Some of the seed fell by the wayside and birds came and ate it. In the second description, some of the seed fell on hard or stony ground that didn't have much soil. The seed did sprout, and actually, it started to grow immediately. But because it lacked depth and no real root system took hold, the sun scorned it, and it withered away. Consider this: trees grow in two directions at the same time. They are both gravitropic and phototropic.

What grows downward, the root system, corresponds to what grows upward, branches and fruit. The work of pushing down through the earth and soil is hard, but it allows what happens above the ground to be free and without restraint. Pruning allows more of the depth to be on display by producing more fruit. In other words, your depth in Christ will reflect your growth in Christ. If you lack roots, you will lack growth. We'll share more on that in a minute.

The story continues with yet another interaction between the seed and the ground. In this seed encounter, some fell among thorns. This time the thorns grew up and dominated the plant, choking it out and preventing it from producing fruit. Lastly, some of the seeds fell on good soil. The outcome was remarkably different. This seed sprang forth and increased, producing in some cases thirty, sixty or even a hundred times as much as was planted. You might wonder, as did Jesus's disciples, if this parable or story was more than an agricultural lesson on growing crops. Scripture indicates that when the disciples and followers were alone with Jesus, they wanted a deeper explanation of this teaching.

So, Jesus explained it this way: The seed represented the Word of God, the truth of scripture. And as it was being shared, the audience that symbolized the wayside ground, were ones that heard it but were under immediate attack from Satan. His agenda was to try to take away completely or at least taint all that they heard with lies and attempts to alternate or manipulate God's truth and His promises. The same tactic he used against Adam and Eve in the Garden of Eden, he still uses today through various cultural movements, the media, and politics. Satan is trying to convince men that they are women and that meaningless casual sex outside of God's marital design is harmless. He wants to disregard and destroy the elderly and the unborn. His plan is to demolish the family and the church.

Next, Jesus teaches that the stony ground group are those that once again heard the Word, seemed to gladly receive it, but because they were not grounded in Christ and lacked roots (depth in the knowledge and understanding of God's Word), their newfound joy and appearance of change was short lived. When trouble arrived on the scene, when hardship and affliction showed up because of the Word of God, they were offended and fell away, abandoning this version of faith. When faced with the suffering that the cross and one's relationship to it would bring, it was no longer worth it to them. We live in times, and there are greater times coming, when the challenge against our faith and the persecution of our beliefs will force people into some consequential decisions about what they stand for and what they are willing to risk continuing to stand on it. Currently, Christians around the world are having to hide and be part of what we refer to as underground churches just to honor their faith in Christ Jesus at the risk of losing everything… including their lives. In America, it has slowly begun and will increase over time, pushing the church to choose protection and compromise over persecution.

And then there's thorns. The ones equated with the thorny ground, like the previous ground types, heard the Word of God. Verse 19 of Mark 4 says that it was the "cares of this world" that caused unfruitfulness. Examples in the same text include: "the deceitfulness of riches" and "the lusts of other things entering in" that strangled any potential growth, productivity or fruit. These lives lacked tangible results as purpose was choked out of them, as focusing on truth was drawn out of them, as a commitment to Christ was distracted by stuff and things. Here's a great self-assessment moment. What distractions are impacting your fruitfulness and your faithfulness? What worldly thing has risen above all heavenly things?

Thorns can be very subtle. Have you ever held a rose and unintentionally poked your finger? We don't always see those things that are poking and pulling us away from our journey with God. It appears our attention spans have shortened over time, and it doesn't take much, any shiny object, to take us off track when it comes to what should be at the core of who we are as followers of Christ. Maybe your job has become that shiny object. Or the pursuit of a relationship has preoccupied your heart. Please don't misunderstand, I'm not saying jobs or relationships are a bad thing. The question is, what occupies your heart? Matthew 6:21 says, "For where your treasure is, there will your heart be also." Your heart will follow after whatever you treasure most.

If we are honest, we'd have to admit that sometimes our thorns aren't as noble as a job or a relationship. James 1:15 states that, "Every man", I believe that includes all human beings, "is tempted when he is drawn away of his own lust and enticed." Enticed means it attracts or tempts us, and in this case, it is our own lust and desires that draw us. Think about what you crave or have an intense desire for. That lust in your heart can be the thorn that leads to your unfruitfulness. And just like thorns, they poke at you, ultimately causing pain and infections in your life. I can't even begin to make a fully comprehensive list, so I need you to take a sincere inward look at your own heart. Pornography, sexual promiscuity, love of money, attempting to control others or feeling a lack of control in your own life, being dominated by your emotions, and laziness, to name a few, can be what chokes the Word of God out of your life.

In this passage, riches are called "deceitfulness". The things of this world can deceive or trick or fool us into making them more important to us than they should be. For instance, many people put their security in their finances, their 401k, their bank statements. Because of that, what got choked out was seeing and knowing God as our security and protection. In the garden of Eden, Satan's deception convinced Adam and Eve to look to self for security by thinking they could replace God with themselves.

> *"Don't plant apple seeds and expect there to be oranges on the tree."*

I'm grateful for the hopefulness at the end of this parable. That there is the prospect of good ground the seed can fall on. Ground that is broken up and ready to accept the Word of God. As God is the one who draws us to Himself, He is the one that, if we allow Him, will prepare our hearts (break up the ground) for the change and transformation His Spirit alone can bring. He grants us the readiness to embrace His truth and receive His gift of grace. Some of that seed fell on good ground and the response was incredible. The God prepared soil, and the watering brought a harvest and yield that far exceeded what was planted. Here's a quick seed lesson. Every seed reproduces after its own kind, from a lesser degree to a greater degree. Don't plant apple seeds and expect there to be oranges on the tree. But you can expect that one apple seed will become a tree filled with apples, each apple containing multiple seeds with the potential for more and more trees.

The seed in this parable gave a yield of thirty, sixty, even a hundred times the increase. Have you ever considered the chain of events that led to your salvation? Who shared the gospel with you, or how did you come to repent and believe in Jesus Christ? Whoever that person was, who shared the gospel with them? And before that, who shared it with that person? And so on and so on all the way back to the original seed, the Word, Christ Jesus Himself. Buried in the grave and like a plant that went down to go up, he rose as the first fruit of resurrection (1 Corinthians 15:23). That is the reproductive increase of the scripture from generation to generation. That is the multiplying power of the gospel of peace. When that excellent seed finds good ground, hearts ready to submit and surrender, the exponential growth is immeasurable.

Chapter Two

A Grain of Mustard Seed

"It is like a grain of mustard seed, which, when it is sown in the earth, is less than all the seeds that be in the earth:" Mark 4:31

Thank you for your patience as I work my way to the central theme of this book. But please allow me to take one more side journey that I think is valuable. Since we were thinking about seed, I want to share about another seed mentioned in this chapter. Verse 31 uses a mustard seed as a picture comparing it to the Kingdom of God. Along with that, we'll take a look at Matthew 17:20, which compares a mustard seed with our faith. Both spiritual parallels are important to the telling of the story later about Christ in the boat.

Let's backup to verse 30 of Mark chapter 4 where the question is asked, "What can we liken or compare to the kingdom of God?" The thought was, how can we get a better picture of something so far beyond our understanding like the Kingdom of God. How can it be simplified to something common to help us get a better grasp of it? To make it as clear as possible, Jesus used the example of a mustard seed.

The best description of a mustard seed is that it is a very small seed. In this passage, it is depicted as "less than all the seeds that be in the earth". Although it starts small, the result is it grows into a large bush, "greater than all herbs", and its branches grow into "great branches". In fact, the branches grow large enough for birds to take refuge under the shadows they create. From small beginnings to great outcomes is the nature of the mustard seed, which makes it the appropriate comparison for the Kingdom of God. As that seed of the Spirit of God gets planted in our hearts (good ground) the harvest is the fruit of the Spirit: love, joy, peace, longsuffering, gentleness, goodness, faith, meekness, and temperance found in Galatians 5:22-23.

When the branches of love spread out they cover all sins (Proverbs 10:12); joy becomes unspeakable (1 Peter 1:8); peace blossoms to surpass all understanding (Philippians 4:7); patience is birthed out of our trials

(Romans 5:3); gentleness is shared with all men (2 Timothy 2:24); goodness and mercy follow us forever (Psalm 23:6); the branches of our faith spread to justify us before God (Romans 5:1); in our meekness, we inherit the earth (Matthew 5:5); the harvest of faith is virtue, knowledge, temperance, patience, godliness, brotherly kindness and charity (2 Peter 1:5-7).

The reaction of this small seed, the implanted truth of the Word of God, establishes a new Kingdom filled with God's new creation. It's a Kingdom that creates shelter for all that are willing to come under it. Psalm 91:1 reads, "He that dwelleth in the secret place of the most High shall abide under the shadow of the Almighty."

The mustard seed is also compared to faith in Luke 17:6. It reads, "And the Lord said, 'If ye had faith as a grain of mustard seed, ye might say unto this sycamine tree, Be thou plucked up by the root, and be thou planted in the sea; and it should obey you.'" Matthew 17 is similar as it also uses a seed to describe faith. "And Jesus said unto them, 'Because of your unbelief: for verily I say unto you, if ye have faith as a grain of mustard seed, ye shall say unto this mountain, Remove hence to yonder place; and it shall remove; and nothing shall be impossible unto you.'" (Matthew 17:20).

Let me be clear, this isn't about us. The focus of our faith should be in what God can do and what Jesus has already done and has promised to continue to do. This is not about you attempting in your strength to relocate Mt. Rushmore or rearrange a forest, it's about believing in the power and might of God to handle every situation you face and supply every need you have. Hebrews chapter 11 says, "Now faith is the substance of things hoped for, the evidence of things not seen." Our hope and faith is in Christ alone.

Here's an illustration I like to use for Hebrews 11:1 is this: if you hope to make a chocolate cake you first need flour, cocoa, eggs, milk, sugar, baking powder, salt, oil and water. They are the ingredients for a cake, the substance if you will. They need to be put together, mixed and blended. Then placed in a baking pan and placed in the oven, all the while you are still hoping the final outcome will be a cake. You have the substance you need for a cake. Now for the evidence. The cake has been in the oven for a while and though you still don't see it, you smell the delicious aroma as it finalizes in the oven. That smell is evidence of what is being prepared in the oven. It confirms that the end result has arrived… a cake.

Faith is what you need for you to walk in the plans and good works God has for you. It is the proof of your relationship with Jesus Christ and the key to your salvation (faith in his grace). Faith is both the substance and the evidence of our journey with Jesus as Lord and Savior. One of my favorite salvation explanation passages of scripture is Ephesians 2:8-10. It says, "For by grace are ye saved through faith; and that not of yourselves: it is the gift of God: Not of works, lest any man should boast. For we are his workmanship, created in Christ Jesus unto good works, which God hath before ordained that we should walk in them."

A grain of mustard seed of faith turns a rejected sibling into a prince of Egypt (Joseph); a baby in the river into a deliverer of Isreal (Moses); a shepherd into a king (David); and an enemy of believers into a pillar of the Christian church (Paul). People are sometimes fooled into thinking they need to come to Christ already strong and secure in their faith. God is more interested in a humble and surrendered heart, with a broken and a contrite spirit, and He'll form you into His workmanship or masterpiece. God will be the one that grows the small seed into something special for the Kingdom.

> *"God is more interested in a humble and surrendered heart…"*

Chapter Three

Let Us Pass Over unto the Other Side

"And the same day, when the even was come, he saith unto them, Let us pass over unto the other side." Mark 4:35

We have arrived at the main theme of this book. I love this particular passage of scripture. We've already talked about the fact that Jesus has been teaching and preaching. He preached a parable about the sower and taught the deeper meaning of the message. He's talked about the mustard seed and one of His reoccurring themes, the Kingdom of God. Now the end of that day arrived, and Jesus says to them, "Let us pass over to the other side." In other words, 'Guys, time to pack up our stuff and get in the boat cause we're going to the other side of the lake.' Let's pause here to consider something. If we believe the word of God, and we believe that Jesus does not do anything that the Father has not shown him and He does not say anything that the Father has not given him to say, then what we can believe is that the Father told Jesus to say this to them.

Next, we must ask if we believe that Jesus only speaks truth. The disciples clearly heard Him, but were they listening? We know they heard Him because they all loaded on the ship, but did they believe the forecast of where this journey would take them. I'm trying not to get ahead of my own thoughts, but the end of the story seems to indicate they heard him, but they weren't listening. Jesus relayed a message from the Father to the disciples, they heard Him, but set it aside. How often do we react just like the disciples? We hear God, but we set aside what He has said. Why? Why do we do that? Maybe you don't, maybe you hear and jump right on everything the Lord speaks to you. Me… I struggle to do that… a lot!

I'm not sure if we hear it and don't believe it or if we hear it and just ignore it. Here's a modern example we may all be able to relate to. Have you ever been scrolling on your phone while someone else is talking to you? And because of what you are focused on, namely your phone, you hear something, but you are not paying it much attention. Often our dialogues with God look like that. He is speaking to us, always something we need to hear, and at times it is a direct answer to your prayers, and our distraction cause us to miss it. Prayer is a two-way communication and conversation; us talking to God and Him listening, and God talking to us and us listening. Us pouring out our heart to Him and, best of all, God pouring out His heart to us.

Frequently, we finish our prayer-talking, give Him our requests and/or list of demands, and then we move on. We skip or ignore the part where God is responding to us. People have often said they have trouble hearing God. My first question is usually, "Are you listening?" Do you listen in prayer? Do you slow down and get quiet with God? Do you listen through the scriptures? Do you listen openly to what He says, not just what you want to hear? One of those reasons is usually why I miss hearing something God is saying to me.

I don't know what was going on with the disciples. It is possible they heard it, accepted it, but never thought the fulfillment of that would be challenged in an adverse way. Sometimes our mind expects an easy path to everything that happens or is supposed to happen in our lives. And when what we expected gets disrupted, we forget what we were promised. For my own sake, I need to repeat that. When we are challenged and thrown off, when what we expected gets disrupted it causes us to forget what we were promised.

> *"Prayer is a two-way communication and conversation; us talking to God and Him listening, and God talking to us and us listening."*

We just established that Jesus only speaks the Father's truth, so we can take what He says as a promise that will come to pass. The statement "Let us pass over" was both directions and a guarantee. Jesus was stating not only what they should do but also what would happen. We cannot allow doubt or fear to arise because of what happens between the directions and the destination. That is where we must cry out, "Lord, increase our faith!" (Luke 17:5).

As much as we'd like to work the process and manipulate the outcome in our favor, in the end, it's not ours to control. Is that your struggle? With every challenge do you say, 'I'll do it as long as it's easy'. 'I'll go, but not alone'. 'I'll agree, but here are my terms'. Because we are so focused on our being in command it is easy to forget what Jesus said as the situation takes an unexpected turn. Let me ask, how do you handle disruptions in your plans? Picture life as a photo album that you are filling with images. How do you handle it when you come to a page you had pre-filled with pictures and now reality doesn't match it?

What we should be doing is putting in the pictures God is giving us in the moment. What usually happens is we run ahead in our mind and place pictures that we want to see and that we expect to happen. Disappointment is simply unmet expectations. When we make concrete plans that don't materialize, we wind up frustrated and dissatisfied. Even when we recognize we have no real power over the outcome of a scenario, we still try to impose our will and our design. The reason is often because we fear the alterative possibilities. We fear we won't like it or can't handle it. Fear is us doubting what God says is true and believing the enemy's false projections. Many have heard this acronym for F.E.A.R., False Evidence Appearing Real. When the Lord has truly spoken a plan for you, we have nothing to fear. We need to remember and hold in our hearts whatever he has said and never doubt.

> *"Disappointment is simply unmet expectations."*

"Let us pass over" is a statement of God's power, sovereignty and control of every situation. Think about it this way, the phrase "pass over" means there are things that you will simply progress beyond. In the Old Testament concerning Moses and the children of Israel, the 'Passover' meant the Lord would pass over the doorpost marked with lamb's blood sparing the first born. For Christians, the punishment of hell and eternal damnation will pass over those sealed and cover by the blood of Jesus. In this circumstance it was the lake they would pass over, but what is it in your life? What does God intend to take you over? There was no promise that there wouldn't be waves or wind. The promise was coming ashore on the other side of the lake. There will be storms that will come to trouble you. You may be blown from side to side, but remember the promises. You don't have to be greater than the lake or the storm. The responsibility for you making it to the end destination rests with the one who made the guarantee.

When it comes to hurricanes, we measure using the Saffir-Simpson Scale with a Category 5 being the worst. Tornadoes use the Enhanced Fujita Scale (or EF Scale) to measure their strength with an EF 5 being the most devasting. What is your Cat 5 or EF 5? What has come in your life leaving you with the fear that you won't get through? And yet Jesus says you will pass over. I'm not saying the trip will be easy, that was not what Jesus promised His disciples. He said they were destined to pass over everything that would come up to stop them.

I faced my Cat 5 storm at my father's bedside as he died from cancer in 1993. I faced two EF 5s when my mother and sister both died from COVID in back-to-back years (2020 and 2021). I have suffered heartache in a broken relationship with one of my children. Wind and rain have blown through my marriage, but through it all God has brought us to the other side of the lake. Truth be told, many days I echoed the attitude of the disciples, and I didn't remember to hold on to the promise that God would never leave me nor forsake me (Hebrew 13:5).

What storms have blown you off course? Maybe it is a fatal diagnosis for you or someone you love. Perhaps it could be financial collapse or loss of employment. Addictions? Legal fights? Has depression been the storm that seemed to fill your boat? We'll examine some of those possible storms in the next chapter. Let me offer this bit of encouragement, if you are reading this book, it's because your boat didn't go under. You may feel shipwrecked as though you are clinging to pieces of wreckage, but let me assure you, help is on the way. You may be frantically bailing water, but I want to confirm that Jesus is right there.

Chapter Four

A Great Storm of Wind

"And there arose a great storm of wind, and the waves beat into the ship, so that it was now full." Mark 4:37

Before we look at the storm, let's set the stage. Jesus has finished teaching and told the disciples we are going to the other side of the lake. Verse 36 adds an extra factor to the equation. "And when they had sent away the multitude, they took him even as he was in the ship. And there were also with him other little ships." Mark 4:36. As we are investigating this storm, keep in mind some others are impacted by your storm. We will revisit that thought later, but I wanted to drop that teaser.

Let's talk about a great storm of wind. There arose a great storm of wind. Wind is the movement of air, and the velocity determines the impact. A light breeze can feel like relief on a hot day, but a tornado can tear your house apart. A great storm of wind can do great damage. Something to keep in mind about the wind is that since it is air it is invisible to the eye. This is how that relates to our text, you can't always see what is affecting you. You can see what the wind is doing as trees bend over, leaves rustle, and waves roll, but you don't see the wind. When you see a tornado, what you are seeing is the dirt and debris caught up in the vortex of the cyclone, but the wind is still unseen. You can see the clouds moving and

> *"Because it's hard to fight what you can't see. It is hard to pray against what you can't identify."*

rotating in the sky, but the wind remains hidden from view. Why is that important? Because it's hard to fight what you can't see. It is hard to pray against what you can't identify. Our storms can be undefined and elusive and even undetectable to our eyes, but the damage is real.

The wind was at the root cause of this storm on the sea. What causes our storms? It can be our own sin, it can be the influence of the broken world around us, or it can be an assault by Satan, our enemy, and the enemy of Christ. Our sin and disobedience can cause storms to rise in our lives. That is the fallout of sin, disruption in the flow of God's presence in our lives. The demonic presence and activity in the world and the brokenness of this existence can come against us to create storms as well. Those worldly storms as well as our sin choices are influenced by the enemy. He is a thief, a liar, and a deceiver. Satan will try to come against us anyway he can. His desire is to kill, steal and destroy all that is good from God in our life (John 10:10)

     How many of you have had a storm in your life? How many of you, out of the clear blue, have found yourself in a downpour and under attack? I was driving the other day, and it was beautiful outside, and it suddenly started raining. I'm looking up and it is a clear, sunny day, but it starts raining to the point where I needed to turn on my wipers. Even in conditions that look sunny and look like there shouldn't be any problems, storms can arise. When it looks like there shouldn't be any cause or reason for worry or concern, suddenly, a storm can occur. Are you battling unmeasurable grief and loneliness? Maybe the storm you are facing is the fear of rejection or the disappointment and damage of actual rejection. You didn't deserve that treatment, but from out of nowhere, the waves come crashing in.

     You can be in a relationship for years and years and years and all seems to be going well. Then, suddenly, the deluge begins. Many of you have been hit with the Cat 5 called divorce. It wasn't what you wanted, you fought as hard as you could to save your marriage, but here you sit with your boat filling with water. You can be raising your children up, loving them and enjoying them, and then suddenly storm winds come blasting in and they want nothing to do with you. You can take from this parable that ready or not, expected or not, prepared or not, storms are going to come. And sometimes they come one storm after another after another after another. I was living in Florida in 2004 when the state was impacted by four hurricanes that year. Three storms hit the area of Florida where I live. We changed from the Sunshine State to the "blue tarp state" or the "plywood state".

You've heard the expression, when it rains it pours. When there is a major storm, the water penetrates and may reveal cracks and damage that was previously unknown. Storms cause roofs to leak. The rain or the 'pain' finds it way in every opening and gap it can access. In the case of the disciples, they experienced a storm with such strong wind that it filled the boat with water. If a boat is full of water, there's a good chance that it's going under. If your emotional boat is full of water, you probably are, or at least feel like, you are sinking. This is where the fear and anxiety set in. Drowning causes panic. When you feel like you are drowning in your circumstances and it is overwhelming you, you become afraid. When you get hit by that kind of storm, you just can't bail that fast. Under your own strength, under your own power, you just can't get rid of the water fast enough or outrun the storm.

Consider this, the boat is full of expert fishermen. This is my speculation, not scripture, but I'm sure they tried everything they could possibly think of to deal with this sudden problem. They may have shifted this and they moved that, they probably unloaded and got rid of as much as they could.

> *"Storms cause roofs to leak."*

They did everything they could think of doing and look at what happened. The storm was still so overwhelming that the waves beat into the ship and now the ship was full. The wind was blowing and causing the water to move. The water was both moving the ship and filling the ship. Everything seemed to be working against them and nothing they were doing could stop it. The text doesn't tell us who it was, but someone finally thought about crying out to Jesus.

Isn't that so typical of us? We exhaust every option in our human thinking before turning to spiritual help. Maybe like us, the disciples didn't want to bother Jesus. Christians struggle more than required because of thinking they would be bothering God with their 'little' problem. We sometimes think we should be mature enough in our spiritual life that we should be able to handle small stuff. We may think God expects us to prove our spiritual level by figuring it out for ourselves. You remember what happened to Adam and Eve when they made up in their own minds that the fruit was worth a bite even though God said not to.

Maybe we think with basic intelligence and common sense we should be able to navigate our troubles on our own. For instance, I'm not against doctors or medicine, but shouldn't prayer come first? Should we be bringing our difficulties and burdens to Lord before taking them anywhere else? Isn't it better to talk to the Lord in prayer instead of complaining to strangers on Facebook?

What will it take in your life to cause you to cry out to the Lord? Because for them it was the only option left. Listen, instead of us seeking Jesus as a last option, I pray that you make it your first choice. They waited till the boat was full to seek Jesus. Where was Jesus? During all this panic and fear and bailing and frustration and splashing and thrashing no one had considered finding Jesus. We'll examine how Jesus was reacting to the storm in the next chapter. But first, do you recall that there were other little ships with them? If they were facing such adversity in the big boat, what were the smaller ships dealing with?

It is easy in your storm to only think about what you are facing. I mentioned the passing of my father as one of my storms. Well, simultaneously, my siblings lost a father, my mother lost a husband, my children lost their Papa, my wife lost a loving father-in-love, our church lost a Pastor and our community lost an amazing man and friend to many. The other ships were impacted by the same storm I was facing. It is hard to come out of your pain to think about others. It is a challenge to work through your pain and help others work through theirs at the same time. I know I shut down for a long time and I wasn't much help to anyone.

I'm not saying it's your fault that others are experiencing this storm, I'm just pointing out that major hurricanes can affect a lot of people. Families have experienced the fallout of sin storms brought on through the choice of an abusive parent. The entire family is impacted by that storm. Children carry the pain of divorces and separations well into adulthood and even into their own newly formed families. Drugs and alcohol have left lasting marks on everyone exposed to it. Even how we treated a store clerk yesterday can be the aftermath of the anger and bitterness we endured in our childhood. Storms, no matter if they originate from around us or begin within us, they can have an impact on others near us.

Think about the fact that while we were suffering with the effects of our sin, Jesus made the ultimate sacrifice and gave his life for our sin. Having been whipped and beaten and nailed to a cross, while hanging there, He cried out to Heaven and said, "Father, forgive them for they know not what they do." (Luke 23:34). During the greatest agony and sorrow, He was thinking about what was happening to us or what would happen to us if He didn't pay this price. Jesus modeled for us the greatest example of love ever. Can we love others through our own pain? Can we come along side of those that are suffering while we are hurting and suffering ourselves? Can we be loving and merciful and usher in healing to others experiencing trauma, even if it's from our storm? Only by God's grace and help.

Finding Jesus amid these matters is our only hope and it's the best hope for all the little ships around us as well. The only way we can heal and help others find healing is in the one called Wonderful, Counselor, the King of Kings and the Prince of Peace. Facing what seemed like the end for them, the disciples sought out Jesus. No matter how great the storm, Jesus is greater. Regardless how the wind is blowing, Jesus is where we need to seek shelter. Psalm 61:3 reads, "For thou hast been a shelter for me, and a strong tower from my enemy." When we find ourselves in a storm, Jesus is both our shelter and our protection.

> *"Can we come along side of those that are suffering while we are hurting and suffering ourselves?"*

Chapter Five

Asleep on a Pillow

"And he was in the hinder part of the ship, asleep on a pillow: and they awake him, and say unto him, Master, carest thou not that we perish?" Mark 4:38

When you squeeze fruit or press an olive, you release the juice or the oil inside. How we respond under pressure says a lot about what's in us. In the midst of the storm, what came out of the disciples was fear. Their words reported what was in their hearts. Scriptures says, "...for of the abundance of the heart his mouth speaketh." (Luke 6:45). Our challenges and trials find the outlet to reveal what is in us. Are you filled with faith or fear? Do you respond to storms based on seeking and trusting the Lord or are you overtaken by anxiousness and worry? How do you react when your life is taking on water? Let's look at the difference in the reaction of the disciples and the response of Jesus.

In 1855, Joseph Scriven wrote a poem to comfort his mother, which has become the beloved hymn, *What a Friend We Have is Jesus*. One of the most powerful stanzas says, "O what peace we often forfeit, O what needless pain we bear, all because we do not carry everything to God in prayer." Whenever I read the story in Mark 4, I think about this song and the peace being forfeited in the panic of the storm. I think about the pain of not carrying our burdens to God in prayer. It is a privilege to carry our sin, our grief and cares to God in prayer.

> *"O what peace we often forfeit, O what needless pain we bear, all because we do not carry everything to God in prayer."*

I am resuming writing this book the day after Hurricane Milton struck Florida (10/10/24) and the eye of the storm passed over where I live in Brevard County. My storm reaction was to be as prepared as possible. We closed the window shutters and put away anything outside that could become flying debris. We made sure to have food and water, as well as candles as a backup in the event we lost electricity. Our cars were filled with gas in case stations ran out. Our home was high enough that we didn't need to surround our doors with sandbags, but others did. We invited a friend and some family to come stay with us because their homes were at greater risk. And yes, we prayed and asked others to pray. Many friends and family reached out concerned about how we would fare during this catastrophic event. Many people evacuated the area, we chose to stay put and "hunker down" to ride out the storm.

    One thing about hurricanes, unlike life storms, is that you can literally see them coming miles away. We were able to watch forecasts and weather tracks to tell where and when the storm would make landfall. My ability to do something to prepare was based on so much advanced warning. But life's storms can come without warning and catch you unaware. The impact of Milton was tremendous. There was major damage scattered across our state and there was even loss of life. This hurricane was so powerful that it spawned a record number of tornadoes. Have you ever had a storm create another storm? When you are facing that, it is understandable that fear would show up. It is often the 'not' knowing that invokes the fear response. The disciples didn't know if they were going to make it. Our usual response to life-threatening situations is to be scared. Had the disciples known a storm of that magnitude was coming, maybe they would have prepared and reacted differently. Even though the storm caught them off guard, the outcome had already been told that they were going to the other side of the lake.

    To finish my storm story, we came out of the hurricane without any wind damage or flooding and never lost electricity. We were truly blessed. We watched the radar as the storm shifted and the shape changed so that on the backside where we were, the rain was much less than predicted. God can alter your storms, but we'll discuss that a little later. Even knowing the storm was coming, it was still devastating for so many. It wasn't that our preparation was better than other people's that experienced damage, storms just do what they do. God's more concerned about our response in the storms and where we look for our true protection. Your life storms will come to wreak havoc any way they can. How will you handle it?

Once the disciples decided to find Jesus, the text seemed to indicate that they found something they didn't expect. While they were fighting for survival, Jesus was asleep. He's not just asleep. He's asleep on a pillow. That's a different kind of sleep. It's one thing to just fall asleep in the chair watching television, I do that often. But when you mean business, when it's time for some serious rest, we usually get a pillow and a blanket. Jesus went into the hinder part of the ship with a deliberate plan to rest. He'd been preaching and teaching all day. He was exhausted and physically drained, and he decided his earthly body needed some rest. So, he went to sleep. Jesus sought out a place in the hinder or back or rear of the ship.

Let me remind you what was going on while he was sleeping. There was a storm going on. Having been there, I understand their question. They came to Him, and they woke him up. And they said, "Master, carest thou not that we perish?" In other words, "We are in the worst storm we've ever experienced, and we think we're not going to make it. We are fighting for our lives and you're sleeping? Don't you care? Does what we are going through even matter to you?"

Can you hear yourself in their response. How many times have you questioned why God was allowing things to happen to you? How often have we doubted if the Lord even cares about our situation? I'm not going to put words into their mouths, but I can image from experience what my thoughts would be. I have said to God in my own way, "Listen Jesus, at least come and grab a bucket and help us." That's our prayer... "Jesus, grab a bucket and start bailing with me. I need you to join me in fixing this my way. I have a plan, so I need you to assist me in my strategy." And I believe God's heart is, "No, I need you to join me. Grab your pillow. I'm not coming to bail water with you, I want you to come rest with me."

In Matthew 11 verses 28 through 30, Jesus says, "Come unto me, all ye that labour and are heavy laden, and I will give you rest. Take my yoke upon you and learn of me; for I am meek and lowly in heart: and ye shall find rest unto your souls. For my yoke is easy, and my burden is light." He wants you to take on His yoke or burden, because it's easy and light, especially compared to what you are carrying. He desired for the disciples to trust Him and find rest in His promises of arriving on the other side. If we trust Jesus enough to cast our cares upon Him, His exchange is to give us rest. 1 Peter 5:7 reads, "Casting all your care upon him; for He careth for you." The way to find out how much God cares, is to give Him your cares. The disciples questioned if Jesus cared, the best way to find out was to release their cares and worries to Him. Listen to Jesus in John 14:27. "Peace I leave with you, my peace I give unto you: not as the world giveth, give I unto you. Let not your heart be troubled, neither let it be afraid." Jesus doesn't want us to be afraid, He wants us to find peace in Him.

> *"The way to find out how much God cares, is to give Him your cares."*

Take a moment and compare the reactions to the storm. The disciples, when confronted by the storm, questioned whether Jesus cared what happened to them. Jesus, during that same storm, was at rest. If as Christians, by the very definition of claiming that title, we should desire to follow the example of Christ. Many dictionaries define being being a Christian as one who professes a belief in the teachings of Jesus. It is so much more than that. To be a Christian, you must make a conscious choice to turn from your sins - that's repentance - and by faith believe that Jesus is the Son of God, who loved us, paid the price of our sins on Calvary's cross, shed His blood and died, was buried, and was raised to life on the third day. A Christian is a person who is born again by the Spirit of God as he or she wholeheartedly trusts in Jesus Christ and seeks to follow Him in obedience.

There is action that follows the faith; the action of living and being like Jesus through His Spirit indwelling and empowering our lives. We are not saved by our works, but our faith produces Kingdom work that glorifies God. Jesus would rather you rest and rely on Him in your storms, than to doubt and become filled with fear. As you commit all that you are to Christ and press into Him, you will find a strength that conquers your fear, His strength. Your new first reactions to storms will be to grab a pillow and rest in Him and with Him, knowing that God is in control. Yes, there may be waves and rough seas ahead, but you need to cling to God's promise of emerging on the other side of the storm.

Chapter Six

Peace, be still

"And he arose, and rebuked the wind, and said unto the sea, Peace, be still. And the wind ceased, and there was a great calm." Mark 4:39

The disciple woke Jesus and immediately questioned His concern for them. Notice Jesus did not answer them or address their concerns, not right away. Let me ask, how many of you think God is not at work when you don't hear Him or see Him moving? How many of you try to force God to be accountable to explain everything He's doing in your life first before He makes a move? We do that, I do that, because in those moments, I only want God to do what I have sanctioned. In the throes of political campaigns, you'll see those commercials where at the end the candidate says, "I'm so and so, and I approved this message." We treat God like He should only do what we have pre-approved. Have you ever stopped to think that God doesn't wait on the approval of someone that doesn't know what to do? I know that may seem harsh but consider that if the disciples could fix their problem, they wouldn't have needed to interrupt Jesus from His nap.

The text says that Jesus "rebuked" the wind. To rebuke is to express strong disapproval because of someone's behavior or actions. The book of Matthew describes another storm that Jesus chose to walk on. In that story, it describes the wind as contrary. It means something is doing the opposite of what you want.

> *"The water was reacting to the wind, the boat was reacting to the water, and the disciples were reacting to the boat."*

This wind was certainly contrary in that it was tossing the ship, creating waves that were about to take the boat under or capsize it, and it was invoking fear in His children. So, Jesus rebuked the wind, then He spoke to the sea. He made it clear that the wind was causing unwanted problems. The water was reacting to the wind and the boat was reacting to the water and the disciples were reacting to the boat. So, Jesus began by addressing the wind. Scripture doesn't tell us what He said to the wind, but I can guarantee He got the wind's attention.

Sometimes God will address our problems before dealing with our reaction to the problem. In Malachi 3:11, the Lord of hosts says he will "rebuke the devourer for your sake." He crushed the serpent's head and dealt with our sin, then attends to us. To show you what I mean, let's look at Romans chapter 5. In the eighth verse it reads, "But God commendeth His love towards us, in that while we were yet sinners, Christ died for us." He clearly showed and proved His love for us by dying for us when we weren't asking and weren't interested. We were still in the depths of our selfish sinful behavior and wicked attitude when He made a way out that we weren't looking for. He dealt with our problem, then invited us into His peace.

Yes, He rebuked the wind, but the water was still stirred up and would continue creating waves for a while longer. If the Lord just speaks to your problem but doesn't speak to you, on your own momentum you will continue to create waves, stir problems, have heartaches, embrace stress, walk in worry, and believe lies. Jesus rebuked the source of the trouble but spoke calm to everything reacting to it. Jesus wants to cool us down from everything that has us fired up. There is a song by Benton Stokes and Tony Woods that says, "Sometimes He calms the storm and other times He calms His child." Even if the storm continues, Christ wants to bring us peace, His peace. Jesus was at peace, asleep on a pillow, during the same storm that had others freaking out. But in this situation, Jesus knew the storm was too great of a distraction for His followers to find their peace, so He decided to deal with the problem first.

The passage points out that Jesus specifically spoke to the sea. Having dealt with the wind, He spoke to the sea and said, "Peace, be still." The disrupting force was handled, now the plan included restoring calm. Isaiah foretold of the one who's name would be the Prince of Peace. Jesus was this child, and His government and peace would increase (Isaiah 9:6-7). No one would ever be better qualified to speak peace into a situation than the Prince of Peace. The same is true of our storms and circumstances. Only Jesus can truly speak peace into whatever conditions we are up against. Sometimes we think peace is the absence of trouble, when in reality, peace is the presence of God.

It is fascinating to consider that even though panic had set in, the disciples had enough wherewithal to count on Jesus to do something. We don't always know what He will do or how He will get us through, but can you hold fast to the fact that He will answer when we call? When you lack peace, He will answer. When you lack hope, He will answer. When you are weighed down under the flood of disappointment and pain, He will answer. Peace is a state of security. When we find our security in Christ, we find our peace. In the storm, the disciples lost all sense of security, so they ran to the most secure place they knew, that was in the presence of Jesus. The Psalmist says of God, "For thou hast been a shelter for me, and a strong tower from the enemy. (Psalm 61:3). Christ alone is our shelter and protection in the midst of the storm.

Let's pause again to get personal for a minute. Look deep within and answer this: Is there a storm raging in or around you that you recognize only Jesus can speak peace to? Maybe I should ask, is there a storm you need Him to speak peace over? Will you seek Him? Will you ask Him? Will you trust Him? And will you obey Him? As Jesus stood face to face with the storm, it became clear who was in control, and it wasn't the storm! The words of Jesus, "Peace, be still", were a command, not a suggestion. When He speaks it over you, do you find peace in those words or has the situation ushered in a level of doubt that makes you think that not even Jesus can help? I'm praying Jesus would speak, "Peace, be still", over whatever you are going through right now. Whether it is a recent calamity or a long-time lingering hurt, I pray you hear His words of peace and that it causes you to be still.

> *"Peace is a state of security. When we find our security in Christ, we find our peace."*

Jesus rebukes the wind and spoke to the sea, "Peace, be still", and it was so. The bible tells us that the wind ceased, it literally stopped blowing, because of its rebuke, and the sea became calm, as a result of the command of Christ to be still. Look at the power in the words of our

Savior. He spoke 'peace', and the source of the problem dissipated. He spoke 'be still', and tranquility was returned. Keep in mind that Jesus was operating in His humanity filled with the Spirit. As we mentioned earlier Jesus was guided to act on what the Father says or does. So, Jesus could make this declaration with authority and with no hesitation because of His faith in the Father. He knew that the Father had power and jurisdiction over everything, which included all creation. Hold that thought until later, we'll come back to that in the next chapter.

The Spirit of Christ produces fruit in our lives. A component of that fruit is peace. It makes sense that the overflow of the fruit in Christ Himself would be peace. Jesus spoke from a place that was part of His nature… peace. His wasn't just hoping for or wishing for peace, He was imparting peace. Jesus was declaring Himself over the storm as only He could. Jesus spoke for the water to be still. Psalm 89 verse 9 says, "Thou ruleth the raging of the sea: when the waves thereof arise, thou stillest them." I hope you really take that verse in. Whenever waves arise, He stills them. Let's go beyond thinking of that just in the natural and consider it in the spiritual. No matter what comes, Jesus can still it. No matter what attack the enemy can bring against you, know and rest in the assurance that all the weapons of our foe will fail because of the sovereignty and power of God (Isaiah 54:7).

The timeline is based on when you are willing to hand it over to Him. Hear me clearly, I'm not saying relationships will be instantly repaired or that cancer will disappear overnight. I believe it can if God chooses to, but my point is that peace can enter in as soon as you open the door. Jesus is knocking, not only to have us open the door to a salvation encounter, but also to allow His peace to be ushered in; to allow joy to fill the house; to experience the weight of fear being lifted and removed. 2 Timothy 1:7 says, "For God hath not given us the spirit of fear; but of power, and of love, and of a sound mind." God doesn't give us fear, so He doesn't want us walking and living in fear. But He does give us peace. John 14:27, which we will cover a little more

> *"Peace, be still. Does your storm need to hear these words?"*

towards the end of this writing, reads, "Peace I leave with you, my peace I give unto you: not as the world giveth, give I unto you. Let not your heart be troubled, neither let it be afraid." Clearly this verse declares that Jesus gives us peace and doesn't want us to be afraid.

Peace, be still. Does your storm need to hear these words? Does your heart need to be quieted and calmed from the thunder of emotional battles? Does your mind long for solace and relief from the seemingly endless attacks? Do you desire the Spirit of Christ to reign in you as the Comforter He promised He would be? Jesus has already spoken "peace, be still" for all time. With every flare up and attack from within and without, just remember, He has already made a provision for you to walk in His peace.

Chapter Seven

Why Are Ye So Fearful?

"And he said unto them, Why are ye so fearful? how is it that ye have no faith?
Mark 4:40

Whew! I'm pretty sure that interjection is not found in our text, but there had to be a feeling of relief in the heart of each disciple. I know coming out of my storms is usually met with a sense of relief from all that built up anxiety and emotion. Having the rain stop and the sun come out assures us that the storm has passed. Things are still wet and dripping, but the clouds have parted, and the downpour has ceased. We all appreciate it when our emotions settle down and our mind stops spinning. Arguably, it would make sense that the shift from a storm that was thought to be their end and demise, to peaceful skies and a calm sea, would cause the disciples to experience a feeling of relief. But Jesus had a different reaction.

> *"Many of us don't go deep enough to get to the 'why'. Jesus always goes deep."*

Our text doesn't tell us that Jesus launched into "Hey guys, is everyone okay?" Jesus doesn't appear to offer hugs of comfort in this moment. Instead, He asks two questions. The first is, "Why are ye so fearful?" Jesus returned to the moment when He was awakened by men who were afraid. I don't want you to think I am taking liberty with the scripture. The text doesn't say the disciples were afraid, Jesus did. In His discernment and assessment of the emotions behind their words, Jesus asked them why they were afraid. The perfect one, Jesus, recognized His followers were brought to a point of fear because of the impact of this storm. When Christ invites us to come to Him (Matthew 11:28), do you think it may have something to do with Him knowing that sometimes we are afraid and don't know what to do?

I mentioned in chapter five, a favorite hymn, that later in that same song says, "Jesus knows our every weakness…". Those lyrics are backed by scripture in Psalm 139:2, which says, "Thou knowest my downsitting and mine uprising, thou understandest my thought afar off." Jesus does know us as much as He knew His disciples. He knows when we are afraid. His disciples were afraid, and they couldn't hide it from Jesus. But His question to them wasn't 'if' they were afraid… but 'why'. Have you ever taken time to assess your own reaction in situations? Have you questioned why you responded with fear or anger? What could be behind the surface display? What were you thinking, or in the disciple's case, what were they forgetting?

Jesus asked the 'why'. Many of us don't go deep enough to get to the 'why'. Jesus always goes deep. He realized the answer He was seeking was more for them than for Himself. They needed to know the 'why'. So, what was He basing His question on? In that situation most of would be afraid. Why is He asking the source of their worry? What is the foundation of their fear? Before we address that, let's look at His second question because I believe the answer covers both questions. The second question He asks is, "How is it that ye had no faith?"

Why are they afraid and what happened to their faith? In the midst of the storm, the disciples question whether or not Jesus even cares about them. And notice, Jesus didn't suggest that their faith was weak or waning, He questioned how it was possible that they demonstrated no faith at all. Since Jesus was convinced that there should have been some display of faith, we have to ask what was that faith supposed to be in? In what was their faith expected to be grounded? Ships and boats carry anchors so that when needed they can be used to grip something solid and unmovable to keep them safe in turbulent waters. The disciples appeared to lack a faith-anchor or at least it wasn't being used to hold them in this storm.

What was Jesus' expectation about the disciple's faith? They had watched Him teach and preach. They saw Him physically heal and cast out demonic spirits. They walked with Him and talked with Him on a daily basis. They observed all there was to know about the claims of this man, so much so, that they left everything to follow Him. Here is the central point of what the Holy Spirit deposited in me about the whole of this text. Jesus simply wanted from them, what He wants from us… to believe. He wanted them to believe He was who He said He was. He wanted them to believe that His words were genuine and honest, and His promises were true. Jesus wanted them to believe Him and remember what He had told them from the start. Jesus wanted their faith to rest in the fact that He had shown them continuous love from day one and no storm could ever change that. It must break Jesus' heart every time we question whether He cares about us.

Can you recall the feeling of someone doubting if they matter to you? Have you ever experienced the pain of rejection when it feels that for all you do to show love, even prove your love, it's still not enough. Jeremiah 31:3 says, "The Lord hath appeared of old unto me, saying, Yea, I have loved thee with an everlasting love: therefore, with lovingkindness have I drawn thee." His love goes so far beyond what we could ever give, and yet, in times of our anxiety and fear, we question His love.

Let's take a quick peek back to the beginning of this adventure. When they were packing up and getting ready to go, what did Jesus say to them? In the second half of Mark 4 verse 25, Jesus says referring to the lake, and I quote, "...he saith unto them, 'Let us pass over unto the other side.'" That's where their faith failed. He had told them that they were about to cross over to the other side of the lake. Those words, His words, should have been enough surety that they would make it all the way across, not drown in the middle.

> *"Why are you so fearful... or full of fear?"*

He didn't say, "Boy, I hope we make it to the other side." He didn't say, "Well, hopefully we'll make it if a big storm doesn't kick up on the way." He didn't even say, "Hey guys, I checked the forecast and there is a storm front moving in that we probably can't make it through, so our best bet is to wait until everything is perfect to sail." That's what many of us want, 'perfect sailing conditions'. Jesus wants us to have faith in Him no matter what. He wants us to believe that if He said we are going to the other side, then rest assured, we are going to the other side.

Think about His first question again, because if they had believed, there would be no reason to be afraid. Why were they so fearful...or 'full of fear'? Because they didn't hang on to His promise and recognize that storm or not, they would have no reason to be afraid. The honest answer to many of our 'whys', is that we didn't trust God. Our fear became bigger than our faith and much like Peter did in another episode on the water, we take our eyes off Jesus and put them on the storm, causing us to go under. Why was there no faith in Jesus on display? Again, it was because they didn't believe what He said or what He could do. Often our storms get so furious and overwhelming that we doubt that anything can be done to save us. We resign ourselves to the worst-case outcome, and then we get angry and blame God for 'our' prediction of our predicament.

We either blame Him, claiming He is cruel and punishing us disproportionately to anything we may have possibly done wrong. Or we think He has abandoned us and apparently doesn't care what happens to us. He becomes in our mind a mean task master or a horrible father. Sadly, that's the only picture of a father some people have, so it's hard to see God as a loving father when things hurt so bad.

The love and promises of God say He'll never leave you or forsake you or fail you (1 Chronicles 28:20 and Hebrews 13:5). So, trust Him and let's go to the other side of the lake together. You may have to ride out some wind and a few waves, but He will always be there with you and for you. And even if your faith feels weak and you get scared, you can, and He wants you to cry out to Him… with boldness. Hebrews 4:16 says, "Let us therefore come boldly unto the throne of grace, that we may obtain mercy, and find grace to help in time of need."

Our faith goes missing when we put it in anything other than Christ. Psalm 76:24 states, "My flesh and my heart faileth: but God is the strength of my heart, and my portion forever." Psalm 56: 3 reads, "What time I am afraid, I will trust in thee." It was never about Jesus expecting the disciples to handle things on their own. He always wanted them to trust Him. God is not grading you on how well you can traverse this life without Him. He wants you to give Him your whole heart and trust Him completely in everything. He will even lovingly help you when you struggle to trust Him. He doesn't give up on you. Don't give up on Him.

Having a moment to ponder His questions, while looking around and recalling all that had just occurred, scripture says the disciples now "feared exceedingly". They were hit with a different kind of fear, one that was the product of a newfound insight and awareness. This wasn't about fearing a storm, this was about being in awe of the one who calmed the storm. Mark 4:41 shares the disciple's reaction to what just happened. It says, "And they feared exceedingly, and said one to another, 'What manner of man is this, that even the wind and the sea obey him?'" The disciples were impressed, to say the least. They had seen Jesus take authority over sickness and disease; they had seen His power on display over demons and evil spirits; but over nature and the very atmosphere itself? This was 'Red Sea parting' level stuff. Even Moses had to rely on God to put His power in the rod… this man 'was' the rod! The rod and staff that comforts (Psalm 23:4), the rod of iron that rules and breaks (Revelation 2:27, Psalm 2:9).

    The disciples realized this 'man' was more than they had comprehended and was even greater than they imagined. I don't know that 'we' fully grasp the magnitude of the power of Christ. Jesus, the Word, was the author of everything. John 1:1-3 declares that "In the beginning was the Word, and the Word was with God, and the Word was God. The same was in the beginning with God. All things were made by him; and without him was not any thing made that was made." The wind and sea obeyed their Creator. Maybe this was one of those lightbulb moments for the disciples and they became conscious of who was in the boat with them. When will the lightbulb come on for us? When will we understand how dire our need for Jesus is?

    Psalm 27:1 states, "The Lord is my light and my salvation; whom shall I fear? the Lord is the strength of my life; of whom shall I be afraid?" This verse keeps us from fear during the storms. When we truly know who Jesus is, and we recognize His power and authority, we can find peace and freedom from fear. When we acknowledge the truth of Christ, and we embrace our relationship with Him with all our heart and soul, we can live a life filled with His presence.

Chapter Eight

The Other Side of the Sea

"And they came over unto the other side of the sea, into the country of the Gadarenes." Mark 5:1

Chapter 5 of Mark concludes the journey across the sea, and as Jesus stated at the start of the trip, they arrived on the other side of the lake. Jesus understood His mission wasn't meant to end in a tragic boat accident on the sea. He had a necessary appointment on a cross. In a similar way, David approached Goliath with total confidence in his victory. Not because Goliath wasn't a formidable challenge, much like the storm, but because of remembering the promise. David had the anointing and promise of God that he would become King of Israel. When he stepped into the ring with the Philistine, David hadn't been crowned King yet. So, he knew his life would not end at the tip of Goliath's sword. Jesus had come to take away the sins of man. That required a cross, not a storm. It is so important to remember what God has spoken into your spirit and through His Word. The assurances of your breakthrough and deliverance as spoken by God, will not come back void or empty.

Isaiah 55:11 says, "So shall my word be that goeth forth out of my mouth: it shall not return unto me void, but it shall accomplish that which I please, and it shall prosper in the thing whereto I sent it." God's Word will accomplish what He pleases and not return to Him empty and short of fulfilling what He has decreed. Think about this as well, since Jesus is the Word of God, He was going to accomplish the Father's will which was the redemption of mankind. Jesus and His disciples made it to the shore on the other side of the sea. Ever wonder what the rest of the ride was like? Was it filled with joy and celebration or awkward silence? The text doesn't tell us, but getting off the boat and putting their feet in the sand had to feel pretty good.

When God speaks peace to your storm, how do you respond? Hebrews 13:15 reads, "By him therefore let us offer the sacrifice of praise to God continually, that is, the fruit of our lips giving thanks to his name."

Jesus is always worthy of praise. Are you thankful? That is a serious question because we often get so caught up in the aftermath of a storm that we neglect to be grateful that the storm is over. We spend so much time complaining about what we just went through that we don't notice where we arrived. I am in no way saying that the disciples didn't have grateful hearts to be safely ashore, I'm simply prompted by the Spirit to remind us to stay in the moment with God. Philippians 3:13-14 states, "Brethren, I count not myself to have apprehended: but this one thing I do, forgetting those things which are behind, and reaching forth unto those things which are before, I press toward the mark for the prize of the high calling of God in Christ Jesus." Our focus needs to move the past and live in the moment with God.

> *"...he had enough of a moment of clarity to run to Jesus and worship Him."*

The point is, don't hang on to the struggles of your past. The enemy tries to use fear in the present as well as fear we carry from the past. If he can't scare you with what is happening right now, he'll bring up a painful memory and try to paralyze you with something you don't want to visit ever again. If we are not mindful, we can get stuck in the storm that has ended as though it is still raining. The Apostle Paul directs us to forget what is behind us, I believe, for that very reason, so we are not stuck living in former fear. I need to remember just enough to keep moving forward and not keep repeating mistakes, but not hang on to so much as to allow my past hurts to make me freeze in my tracks. Jesus had to get on with His mission, because there was another appointment waiting for Him when He landed.

"And when he was come out of the ship, immediately there met him out of the tombs a man with an unclean spirit, who had his dwelling among the tombs; and no man could bind him, no, not with chains:" Mark 5:2-3. No time elapsed before Jesus was back on assignment of setting the captives free (Luke 4:18). This man from the tombs was embroiled in a battle with an unclean spirit. I call it a battle because the text suggests that even though this man had been chained to try to control him, which didn't work, and that he lived in the mountains and the tombs cutting himself, he still had enough clarity to run to Jesus and worship Him.

The storm crushing power of Christ was recognized by the demons causing them to cry out for Jesus to leave them alone and not torment them. They even acknowledged that He was the Son of the Most High. James 2:19 verifies that the demons know who Jesus is. "Thou believest that there is one God; thou doest well: the devils also believe, and tremble." They know and they tremble. Jesus also knew them and called out that unclean spirit. Jesus required the demon to identify who he was, and he said, "My name is Legion, for we are many" (Mark 5:9). Just for a frame of reference, a Roman military legion was comprised of between 3000 and 6000 soldiers. The point being, this man was struggling and battling a lot of demons. It's hard to imagine the storms he was encountering on a daily basis. The internal turmoil must have been overwhelming and tremendous. Have your storms been like this?

I believe scripture supports that true believers cannot be possessed by a demon, but we are under attack and can choose to fall under the influence and cooperate with the demonic. We can leave doors open and give access to the schemes and tricks of the enemy, but being filled with the Spirit of God gives you the power to be victorious. Don't believe Satan's lies, know and walk in the truth of scripture. Don't dabble in the occult, be free and set apart in Christ. Don't align yourself with the evil works of darkness but be light and salt in the world. When clouds roll in, the first thing they do is block the light. That has always been the plan of the enemy, to block the Light. Those storms try to skew our view of the Light of the world, Jesus Christ, and leave us in a place of darkness.

> *"When clouds roll in, the first thing they do is block the light."*

Our man from the tombs needed what Jesus had to offer… peace. This story requires a deeper examination, but to summarize the conclusion, Jesus cast out the demons and sent them into a herd of about 2000 swine that ran down a hill and drown in the sea. So, the people that had been feeding the swine went and told everyone they saw about what had happened. When the townsfolks came out to see Jesus, they saw the one 'that was possessed with the devil, and had the legion, sitting, and clothed, and in his right mind: and they were afraid.' Mark 5:15. So afraid in fact, that they asked Jesus to leave. People tend to react in different ways to Jesus. Some receive Him and some reject Him. Some love Him and others hate what He represents and how He challenges their control over their lives.

So as Jesus returned to the ship, our nameless friend from the tombs wanted to go with Him. Clearly, no one felt a need to warn him about the potential storms that might await them on the lake. I really don't think it would have mattered considering the storm he was just released from. He was focused on the one that set him free, and he wanted to stay with Him. Interesting enough, Jesus didn't allow him to accompany them on the journey. Why? Look at verse 19: "Howbeit Jesus suffered him not, but saith unto him, 'Go home to thy friends, and tell them how great things the Lord hath done for thee, and hath had compassion on thee.'" Jesus sent him on an evangelical crusade that started in Decapolis spreading the good news of God's love and compassion. And what a marvelous witness he would be! Have you shared your storm deliverance story with others? Have you shared about the compassion God has shown in your life? Have you implored others to seek the peace in the storm that is available in Christ?

I'm going to wrap up this chapter on what I consider a humorous note. After fulfilling this God appointment and ordaining the tomb evangelist, Jesus got back in the boat and went back across the lake! I smile wondering what the disciples were thinking getting back on the ship. My hope for everyone reading this book, is that they will exit their storms with the confidence that Jesus can take them through anything else they might face in the future. The passage doesn't tell us how the return trip went. All we know is that as they were getting close to landing, people were already gathering to see Jesus, one of which was Jairus, with a daughter on the brink of death. As Jesus was pressed by the crowd on the way to Jairus' house, He encountered a woman with a 12-year blood issue. Jesus clearly had some extraordinary appointments awaiting Him back on the other side of the lake. I encourage you to read the passage on your own. Maybe we'll cover that together another time.

Chapter Nine

My Peace I Give unto You

"Peace I leave with you, my peace I give unto you: not as the world giveth, give I unto you. Let not your heart be troubled, neither let it be afraid." John 14:27

At the heart of this message is finding the peace that only comes from Jesus Christ, even in storms. Jesus delivered peace on the boat and that was of great benefit to the disciples. But what about us? It is wonderful to rest in the fact that although Jesus returned to be at the right hand of the Father, He left His peace for us. In John 14 verse 27 it says, "Peace I leave with you, my peace I give unto you: not as the world giveth, give I unto you. Let not your heart be troubled, neither let it be afraid." The verse begins by saying that Jesus not only leaves us His peace, but he gives it to us as well. There is a difference between someone leaving something for you that you still have to go and claim, versus someone placing it in your hand, or in this case, a spirit deposit. Galatians 5:22-23 says, "But the fruit of the Spirit is love, joy, peace, longsuffering, gentleness, goodness, faith, meekness, temperance: against such there is no law."

Upon salvation we receive an imparting of the Holy Spirit, of which a portion of the fruit is peace. Jesus gives us His peace through His Spirit. To have true peace, the only genuine path is the road that leads to a relationship with Jesus. The peace that Jesus gives is unique and distinctive. It is transformative on every level. It impacts more than just feelings and emotions; it grants you spiritual tranquility and peace of mind. The peace of Christ is different from the peace most seek in the world. The world thinks of peace as it relates to the absence of war or a cessation of hostility. Unfortunately, believers are in an ongoing spiritual battle. The world views peace as a time of harmony and freedom from conflict. Followers of Christ have His peace even in trials and tribulations. Jesus says, "I have said these things to you, that in me you may have peace. In the world you will have tribulation. But take heart; I have overcome the world."

In Christ, and I know I keep saying that, but that is the only solution for what we face, we are overcomers and conquerors. Romans 8:37 states, "Nay, in all these things we are more than conquerors through him that loved us." Through Him we go beyond just conquering, we are 'more than conquerors.' How are we more than conquerors? A conqueror defeats an enemy usually after some intense battle. Our enemy was defeated, and we didn't even have to lift a finger. The Lord fights our battles and is always victorious... giving us the victory through Him. That's how we are more than conquerors!

The world connects our peace to how we feel, whether we are happy or sad. The bible bases our peace on being content and resting in Christ. Christ makes contentment accessible through the cross. Psalm 100 offers a beautiful picture of what a life of contentment looks like. "Make a joyful noise unto the Lord, all ye lands. Serve the Lord with gladness: come before his presence with singing. Know ye that the Lord he is God: it is he that hath made us, and not we ourselves; we are his people, and the sheep of his pasture. Enter into his gates with thanksgiving, and into his courts with praise: be thankful unto him, and bless his name. For the Lord is good; his mercy is everlasting; and his truth endureth to all generations." We can serve with gladness and enter into His gates with thanksgiving and praise. All the while knowing that He is good, and that His truth endures generation after generation. You can pass on your contentment as an inheritance.

He closes the verse by directing us that in His peace, we don't need to be troubled or afraid. In the boat the disciples were both troubled and afraid. The wind and the waves had them afraid, and whether or not Jesus cared about them had them troubled. Giving us His peace is His remedy to feeling distressed or anxious. It is the alternative to allowing fear to take over and consume or control us. He says, "Let not" which means you have a choice of what you will consent to or accept. Faith or fear, trust or disbelief, peace or discontentment...you can choose the route your heart travels. You can 'let it' or 'let not' when it comes to receiving or refusing God's peace.

The disciples had a choice just as you have a choice in your storm. Do you press into Christ and permit His power to take over and guide you through to the other side, or do you panic and try to manage it within your own capacity? His peace awaits all those that will put their trust in Him. How does the world give peace? It gives a fake sense of peace that is temporary and surfacy and is in reality just an illusion of real peace. Fake peace tries to calm emotions but doesn't deal with the actual problem. Fake peace attempts to satisfy and appease others around you but doesn't look to honor God. Fake peace can still leave you troubled and afraid.

The problem with fake peace is this: let's say we believe that more money will make us secure, is there a time when we actually feel secure that it's enough money? Or if our security is in our beauty and appearance, what happens to that security as begin to age? What happens to our security in people when people turn against you?

Our salvation in Christ Jesus gives us a security that brings with it peace. The relationships you feel the most secure in, gives you the most peace. If your marriage is functioning in the manner God intended, that security translates to a peace about your relationship. It also becomes the safe haven of peace when other parts of your life seem turbulent. That example is what our walk with Jesus is supposed to be, a place of security and a haven of peace. That connection with Christ needs to be your primary source of peace to weather all the storms you face.

> *"Fake peace tries to calm emotions but doesn't deal with the actual problem."*

Jesus has done everything required for His peace to be available to you. He is offering it to you, will you take it? Consider the alternative of driving winds and rain. Reflect on the results of waves that fill your boat. Wouldn't you rather embrace His peace? Now would be a good time to acknowledge your need to Him. Confess and turn from your own methods to resolve things and ask Him to take the lead. Proverbs 3:5-6 encourages us to, "Trust in the Lord with all thine heart; and lean not unto thine own understanding. In all thy ways acknowledge him, and he shall direct thy paths."

Chapter Ten

The Peace of God and Peace with God

"And the peace of God, which passeth all understanding, shall keep your hearts and minds through Christ Jesus." Philippians 4:8

"Therefore, being justified by faith, we have peace with God through our Lord Jesus Christ:" Romans 5:1

    As we have reflected throughout this book on peace in the midst of the storms of life, we need to consider one last aspect of peace. I know we all want peace from our storms, and we all want a break from our problems. But the peace you are seeking can only truly exist through the peace 'of' God and by having peace 'with' God. Philippians 4 tells us that there is a peace that belongs to God, that goes beyond our understanding. That peace will keep or hold or secure both your heart, and your mind, through or in Christ Jesus. "And the peace of God, which passeth all understanding, shall keep your hearts and minds through Christ Jesus." Philippians 4:8.

    Have you ever seen peace that goes beyond our understanding in action? Have you witnessed or experienced a calm that seems unbelievable in an indescribable tragedy? Or forgiveness in extreme woundedness? Or love in the face of insults and highly volatile hatred? The peace of God can emerge as a presence of God's love and grace that can defy any rational thinking. That's the power of Jesus Christ. His joy becomes our strength (Nehemiah 8:10), a strength that allows us to stand when everyone else would have fallen.

    I've heard this phrase used in conjunction with our country's military leadership and presence on the world stage as 'peace through strength'. I believe that means that as we are seen by the world as militarily strong, that serves as a deterrent and discouragement for our enemies. They foresee the futility of attacking us because it will lead to total annihilation and defeat. That deterrent allows us to exist in a period of no war and no conflict. We have 'peace through strength' in Christ Jesus. Our enemy knows he is defeated and try as he might, when we stand strong in the peace of God, he cannot bring us down. The peace of God goes past our capacity to understand, with our human logic, the effect and impact it can have on our lives. It changes everything. That's the power of God's love towards us. He can hold us and keep us when nothing else can with a strength that nothing else possesses. His love, grace, mercy and peace are beyond incredible!

"Therefore, being justified by faith, we have peace with God through our Lord Jesus Christ:" Romans 5:1. It is the peace of God that draws us and brings us to a place of peace with God. We spoke in our opening about salvation by grace through faith in Jesus Christ. That is what brings us to a place of 'peace with God'. Peace with God means we are no longer enemies or adversaries with God. There is a termination to the clash between us and God for lordship of our lives. We've surrendered our lives to Him.

> "We have 'peace through strength' in Christ Jesus."

There is no longer a battle for supremacy of wills, we have agreed that His will reigns supreme in and over our lives. We are at peace with God because we no longer serve sin, we serve Him alone.

Our faith in Jesus has allowed God to justify us releasing us from the fate of sin, and granting us the gift of eternal life based on His standard. God is both just and the justifier (Romans 8:33). His glory and majesty require that rebellion against His will (sin) must be punished, and that punishment is death or eternal separation from Him. But praise be to God, He is also the justifier that has set the conditions of our exoneration from the punishment of sin through our faith in His Son Jesus and the finished sacrifice Jesus made on the cross of Calvary. When we repent and believe in God's son, we have peace with God. The verse in Romans says that peace comes through Jesus Christ.

We cannot achieve peace with God in any other way, not as the world gives it, not by our own devises or plans... nothing else but Christ Jesus makes that kind of peace possible. The best of all scenarios is to have the peace of God and peace with God. God always wants us to have peace. The book of John describes a scene where eight days have passed after Jesus' death and resurrection and the disciples had gathered in a room with the door shut and Jesus suddenly appears in their midst. His first words to them were, "Peace be unto you." Even when things shock and surprise us or catch us off guard, Jesus always offers peace. He wants us to welcome the peace of God and be at peace with God.

The Lord invites us to be peacemakers in the world around us (Matthew 5:9). Romans 12:18 says, "If it be possible, as much as lieth in you, live peaceably with all men." Ephesians 4:3 tells us we should be "Endeavouring to keep the unity of the Spirit in the bond of peace." As ambassadors of Christ, we must be ambassadors of peace. Since God is the God of peace (Romans 15:33) and Jesus is the Prince of Peace (Isaiah 9:6) and the fruit of the Spirit is peace (Galatians 5:22), so to represent all three, we must demonstrate peace. It is our duty to live in peace, walk in peace, extend peace, and speak peace.

Our mustard seed faith, planted in good soil, brings a harvest of storm-overcoming peace. The Word of God implores us to… "walk by faith, not by sight." (2 Corinthians 5:7). We cannot get distracted by the winds and waves and take our eyes off of Him and His peace. We must have faith in His promises to get us through whatever we encounter. The main challenge of this book is to believe what God said before the storm, while we are in the storm, so we can testify about it after the storm. That happens through the peace of God, and it puts us in the place of peace with God.

Epilogue

There is a very simple fact, we all face storms. Please know that I understand that storms can be painful and devastating. In no way am I minimizing your experience, just offering you hope. The disciple's fear was real and even understandable, but Jesus wants so much more for us. He wants us to experience what His peace is like in every area of our lives. My prayer is that you gain a new freedom walking in the plan of Christ through your traumas and tragedies.

The Word of God goes so much deeper than I can unravel, I am just grateful for the crumbs that fall from His table that I can share with others. My greatest encouragement is to direct you back to the word of God. God will speak insight to you directly through His Word that I didn't capture on these pages. He will write on your heart in ways that I couldn't begin to fathom. But if my words, as I listened to His Word, were in any way a blessing to you, I am grateful. Please pass this along in hopes of blessing someone else. As you read this your mind may have drifted to a friend or family member adrift and being battered by one of life's storms. Ask Jesus to speak 'peace, be still' over them and their situation and offer this book as support and encouragement to build them up along the way.

Most times it seems we are heading into a storm, in the middle of a storm, or coming out of a storm, but in all three moments God's peace remains within reach. I don't want to view life only through the storm lens and become a storm chaser, I praise God for the days when the clouds part and the sun shines through. I desire more of those days than the other kind. It's just a comfort to know that I have a pavilion during the deluge that will protect me and offer me peace. Peace, be still are the spoken words of the grace of God in your time of need.

Lastly, I want to consider the storm damage after a life hurricane hits and moves on. Many of us live out of pain from our past. Like the wreckage left behind by Helene and Milton, we don't always know where to begin to sort things out. It can feel like we've lost everything, and things will never feel normal again. After those life storms, we feel like we could never love again, or trust again, or even smile again. Everything we see reminds us of the hurt or the loss. As we watch others enjoy living, we feel a longing to have that joy and peace in our heart and soul. You may have even asked or considered, 'will this ever end… is there anything to live for?' Some Christians caught in the debris and ruins of the aftermath of a storm, pray and cry out for Jesus to return soon to get them out of this hurt and despair. Well, He is here.

God has not forgotten you. His love for you is as strong and perfect as ever. He knows it is too much for you to bear, that's why He wants you to give it to Him. Let Him carry your pain and if necessary, even carry you for a while, to get you to the other side of your heartache and tears. He wants to bind up your wounds by pouring out a full measure and expression of His unending love for you. He is just a surrendered tear away; He is closer than you think. We often picture Heaven and Jesus way beyond the clouds seemingly out of reach. The truth is, He is a whispered prayer away. He is as near as you turning your thoughts to Him. In 1922 Helen Lemmel wrote, "Turn your eyes upon Jesus, look full in His wonderful face. And the things of the world will grow strangely dim, in the light of His glory and grace." Turn to Jesus and allow Him to speak 'peace, be still'.

Made in the USA
Columbia, SC
07 February 2025

52704985R00033